The Spider Who Never Gave Up

by

Travis Flores

First published by AuthorHouse 09/21/04

ISBN: 1-4184-0337-7 (sc)

This book is printed on acid-free paper.

authorHOUSE

1663 LIBERTY DRIVE, SUITE 200
BLOOMINGTON, INDIANA 47403
(800) 839-8640
www.authorhouse.com

A Wish Comes True

I'm so excited, I can not wait!
My book will be out, around this date.
April is the month, yes in the spring,
Also the month I turn thirteen.
The months go by, the day nears
I am so anxious, but have no fears.

So many people involved with this
such as the terrific Make-A-Wish!
I have an illustrator, she is so cool,
her name is Michelle, her drawings rule!
David and Leslie, their job is so fine,
working for GreenShag Marketing & Design.

So, now you know about this awesome thing
Sparkey and I say thanks for reading!

By: Travis Flores - 1/28/04
Copyright 2004 by Travis Flores

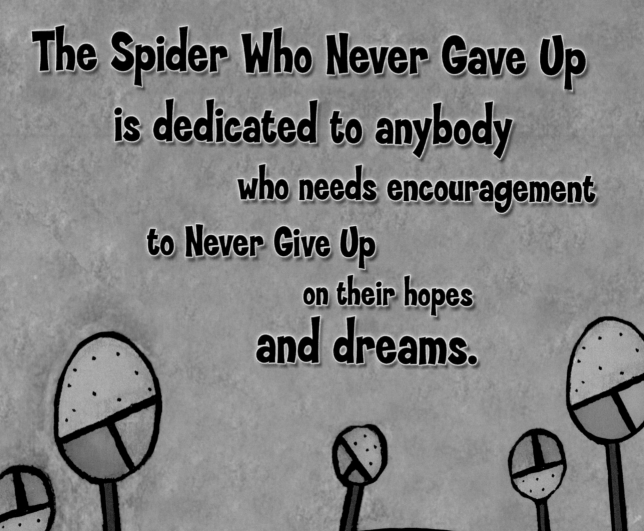

The Spider Who Never Gave Up
is dedicated to anybody
who needs encouragement
to Never Give Up
on their hopes
and dreams.

The Spider Who Never Gave Up! ©1999

Travis Flores.........................Author

Michelle Ciappa...........................illustrator

David Vance............................Design & Art Editor

Michael Moretto...........................Photos

GreenShag Design..................Production Management

One hot summer day,
there lived a spider
named Sparkey.

Sparkey was not an
ordinary spider.

He did not know
how to spin a web.

"Man, oh man, oh man! I've tried and tried, but my web just won't come out right," Sparkey said.

"What's the matter honey?" asked Sparkey's mother curiously.

"Well you see, I can't spin a web!" Sparkey replied.

"Oh dear," his mother said, "take a break and come in for dinner."

"But I can't give up!" said Sparkey.

"I'm not saying to give up, I just think that you need to take a break. After all, you have been working on your web since this morning," his mother said.

"Well okay," Sparkey said,
    "but what are we having for dinner?"

His mom said with excitement,
                        "Stir-Fly!"

The next morning Sparkey
woke up real early and said
over and over to himself...
"I CAN do it!
I CAN do it!"

After a while of trying hard to
spin his web, Sparkey began to cry,
"I just can't do it,"
"I'll never be able to spin my web."

When his mother heard him say this
she barked,
"Never say never, Sparkey
...NEVER!"

"But, but....," replied Sparkey.

Sparkey's mom wouldn't let him talk.
"I was the same way
when I was your age."

"You were?" Sparkey Whined.

"Yes," she said, "just give it some time."

"Fine." Sparkey replied.

Sparkey never gave up.
He worked hard on spinning
a web for years.

"I DiD iT!" Sparkey exclaimed,
"I DiD iT!"

By the time Sparkey was 12,
he could spin a web better
than anyone had ever seen.

Sparkey's mom proudly said, "I told you if you just gave it some time, you would be able to spin a perfect web."

"If you are like me folks, Here's a hint! Go all the way! Don't stop and whatever you do...

Never...Ever give up

on what you want to do – or on your dreams!"

About the Author

Born in April 1991, Travis Flores is an extraordinary young man that has already endured more at his young age than most people do in their entire life. He battles Cystic Fibrosis, a genetically inherited illness for which there is no cure...YET!

However, Travis doesn't let his disease stop him. He enjoys spending time with his family, racing go-carts, playing basketball, riding his bike, and playing the piano and the trumpet. His God-given talent is writing, where he writes poems, short stories and scripts for plays. He was first inspired to write at the age of six when his mom was diagnosed with melanoma cancer and his grandpa was lost to lung cancer. Travis felt that he could best express his feelings by writing.

Photo by Terry Flores

Soon he noticed that people where inspired by his writings. From this, Travis decided to write "The Spider Who Never Gave Up" to give encouragement to others, especially children. He wanted them to know that no matter how bad things may get in their life, they have to keep hopeful and never give up! He decided it could be a GREAT opportunity if he used his "wish" with the Make-A-Wish Foundation® to help publish this story – a wish that keeps on giving because the people that read Travis' story will be touched by his hope and encouragement.

Be sure to visit www.sparkeythespider.com

Additional Writings by Travis

Why is it me?

Sometimes I wonder
Why is it me?
Why is it me,
who has Cystic Fibrosis,
a terminal disease?

Why is it me?
I think God
made me a special plan.
I guess that could be easy
enough to understand.

But, why is it me?
Why do I have to live
with a disease?
With God's help
I'll try to fight,
this horrible disease
with all my might.

So, why is it me?
I don't know.
We'll just have to
wait and see.

By: Travis Flores - 6/14/02
Copyright 2002 by Travis Flores

Dear God, Thanks

Dear God, I just wanted to say thanks
for what you've given me.
A Mom and Dad, both loving as can be.

Dear God, I just wanted to say thanks
for the good times and memories I've had.
You've blessed me with your hands and I'm very glad.

Dear God, I just wanted to say thanks
for the things you do through me.
Writing these poems of inspiration is a God given ability.

So God, I love you and Thanks!

By: Travis Flores - 11/6/03
Copyright 2003 by Travis Flores

God

God sends his angels to us
and they hold us tight.
Protecting us from bad things
that come into their sight.
God is very kind
with one brilliant mind.
He snuggles into hearts,
he's not hard to find.
God is like a factory,
he works in so many ways.
Building up new children
with hearts brighter than sunshine rays.
So now you understand him,
miracle worker, it's true.
Spreading all the love through hearts,
quicker than saying, "God, I love you!"

By: Travis Flores
Copyright 2003 by Travis Flores

The Flores Family

Tim, Terry, Justin, Travis, and Brandon Flores

The Flores family is one of great support to each other and as a group we have learned to Never Give Up. With Travis' diagnosis of Cystic Fibrosis in August of 1991 and his mom's diagnosis of stage III malignant melanoma cancer in April of 1997 we had no choice but to choose perseverance.

Tim is the manager of McClinton Chevrolet's Auto Outlet in Parkersburg, WV. Terry is very busy trying to keep the family

healthy, happy, and active. Justin, 15 years old, basically a straight-A student and is very active in baseball, basketball and go-kart racing. Brandon, 10 years old, an A/B student, likes riding bikes, hiking, swimming, and playing spy & army games with his friends.

Travis, 13 years old, also an A/B student, enjoys writing, racing go-karts, acting, biking, basketball, playing the piano, and hanging out with friends.

Travis's "extended family" also plays a vital role in his life. This extended family not only includes his many relatives and friends throughout the US, but also the entire staff of Cincinnati Children's Hospital Medical Center in Ohio, which at times has been his home away from home. Thanks to all!

Flores Racing

Travis and his brothers have been racing for several years in the Mini Wedge Racing Association. Travis & Justin have won many trophies in the mid-Ohio Valley while Brandon helps his dad in the pits by keeping the carts clean & ready to race. Racing has always been an adventure and has taught us the importance of perseverance. Most importantly, racing gives Travis an outlet from thinking about his Cystic Fibrosis while he is at the track.

We would especially like to thank our sponsors and all the people that make racing possible for Travis and the Flores Family. They have made an incredible positive impact on Travis' life. We really appreciate the great support they have given us on and off the track over the years.

Photo by Michael Moretto

Winning

1 lap, 2 laps, 3 laps more.
Racing that go-cart, harder then before.
Go! Go! Go! Everyone screams.
As the checkered flag drops
and your in the lead.
Yes! Yes! Yes! You say out loud.
As everyone comes over in one big crowd.
Clapping, cheering, hooray's too!
As you win your first race,
Everyone cheers for you.

By: Travis Flores - 4/12/02
Copyright 2002 by Travis Flores

Thanks to Make-A-Wish

The Make-A-Wish Foundation® grants the wishes of children with life-threatening medical conditions to enrich the human experience with hope, strength, and joy. It is the largest wish-granting charity in the world, with 75 chapters in the United States and its territories and 27 international affiliates on five continents. With the help of generous donors and more than 25,000 volunteers, the Make-A-Wish Foundation has granted more than 110,000 wishes to children around the world since 1980. For more information about the Make-A-Wish Foundation, visit www.wish.org.

Thanks to UAW-GM

Travis' wish has been made possible thanks to the generous support of UAW-GM.

Together, the International Union, UAW (UAW-GM) and the General Motors Corporation (GM) are committed to the largest sponsorship in the history of the Make-A-Wish Foundation and have helped grant thousands of children's wishes all across America.

In support of this sponsorship, UAW-GM people, GM employees and GM dealers in communities around the country have personally committed to volunteerism, fund-raising and wish-granting...truly making smiles standard equipment for Make-A-Wish children.

UAW-GM's support comes from the UAW-GM Center for Human Resources, which develops and administers education, training and retraining programs and joint activities for approximately 130,000 UAW-represented GM employees.

Thanks to Michelle Ciappa

"It's been a wonderful experience working with Travis. I was amazed by his positive attitude and how determined he was to make this book happen. I hope to work with him again in the future. I didn't realize my illustrations could make someone so happy. Thanks, Travis. I'm so glad I could be a part of your wish."

Michelle Ciappa is an accomplished illustrator complete with a Bachelor's degree from the Columbus College of Art and Design. Also a graphic designer for 6 years, Michelle's illustrations are quirky, colorful and unique. Originally from Buffalo, New York, Michelle currently lives and works in Columbus, Ohio.

For more information about Michelle's work, please visit: www.meshell-illustrates.com or email her at:thespicyitalian@hotmail.com

Thanks to GreenShag Design

Greenshag Design & Marketing Group is proud to be a part of Travis' wish. Since 2002, GreenShag has created all of the design and marketing materials for the Central Ohio chapter of the Make-A-Wish Foundation®. When we were approached by Make-A-Wish to become such an integral part of this wish we were thrilled.

GreenShag Design was started by David Vance in 1998 and joined by Leslie Neal-Jenkins in 2001. Combining David's expert design and production skills and Leslie's strong marketing and design abilities, GreenShag continues to be the advertising agency of many organizations and businesses throughout Columbus, Ohio and nation wide.

Please visit us at www.greenshagdesign.com or call 614.261.9905 for more information.

Special Thanks to...

Battle Against Cystic Fibrosis

With its slogan, "It's more than just a game...it's a battle for a cure," the B.A.C.F. Ohio vs. West Virgina All-Star High School football game is played each year in Parkersburg, WV near Travis' home area. Since its inception in 1994, the B.A.C.F. has raised more than $100,000 for Cystic Fibrosis research. The volunteers and sponsors of the annual football game (and now basketball, too!) are proud of the work that Travis has done for all of the children stricken with CF. If you would like to help the B.A.C.F. with its on-going work, you may call (800) 795-9188.

The American Cancer Society

The American Cancer Society is the nationwide community- based voluntary health organization dedicated to eliminating cancer as a major health problem by preventing cancer, saving lives, and diminishing suffering from cancer, through research, education, advocacy, and service. Headquartered in Atlanta, Georgia, the ACS has state divisions and more than 3,400 local offices.

At 1-800-ACS-2345, trained cancer information specialists are available 24 hours a day, seven days a week to answer questions about cancer, link callers with resources in their communities, and provide information on local events. The website for the ACS is www.cancer.org.

Flores Racing #43 Sponsors

The Auto Outlet - Parkersburg, WV
Jerry Wagner - Wagner Metro Tire - Parkersburg, WV
Brian K. Carr - Attorney at Law - St. Mary's, WV
Pro-Hardware/Radio Shack - St. Marys, WV
Rubi's Pizza E' Grill - Parkersburg, WV
Mid-Ohio Valley Widetrackers - Parkersburg, WV
339 Speedway - Barlow, OH
For sponsor information, please contact
Tim Flores (304) 865-6500

A special thanks to **David Justus** at Make-A-Wish® for being Travis's Wish Coordinator and helping to make his dreams come true.

Special Thanks to...

The Utah Valley Institute of Cystic Fibrosis

The Utah Valley Institute of Cystic Fibrosis (UVICF) is dedicated to the amelioration of cystic fibrosis through education and research. The institute disseminates the latest findings in cystic fibrosis research to CF patients and their families, as well as hosting a website where more information can be gleaned. The institute is also concerned with funding research of therapies that may not be appealing to large pharmaceutical companies or funding agencies, focussing primarily on translational research that offers the chance of bringing into practice treatments that may be effective in helping CF patients -- regardless of whether the treatments are patentable or profitable. This was the genesis of the Insitute's involvement in researching the use of glutathione as a possible treatment for CF. The UVICF is a non-profit tax-exempt charitable organization, and more information on it may be found at http://members.tripod.com/uvicf/index.htm or you can write to the UVICF at 592 East 200 North, Orem, Utah 84097

The Cystic Fibrosis Foundation

Cystic fibrosis (CF) is a life-threatening, genetic disease affecting approximately 30,000 individuals in the United States and for which there is no cure. A defective gene causes the body to produce an abnormally thick, sticky mucus, due to the faulty transport of sodium and chloride (salt) within cells lining organs such as the lungs and pancreas. The thick CF mucus leads to chronic lung infections and also obstructs the pancreas, preventing enzymes from reaching the intestines to help break down and digest food.

The mission of the Cystic Fibrosis Foundation is to assure the development of the means to cure and control cystic fibrosis and to improve the quality of life for those with the disease. For more information on CF, call (800) FIGHT CF or visit the CF Foundation's Web site at www.cff.org.

For more information about Travis or any of these organizations please visit Sparkey's website at

www.sparkeythespider.com

Sparkey's Fun Pages

Word Find

Find all the hidden words from the story.

SPARKEY
TRAVIS
WEB
HOPE
DREAMS
ENCOURAGEMENT
SPIDER
STIR-FLY
MAKE-A-WISH
GREENSHAG
ILLUSTRATOR
FAMILY
LOVE
POEMS
FOUR-T-THREE
NEVER

M	G	R	M	A	K	E	A	W	i	S	H	L	B	U
V	R	E	F	F	N	N	B	R	N	K	U	O	F	T
H	E	S	P	O	E	E	H	R	R	O	W	V	R	S
U	E	P	O	U	N	V	O	E	S	O	L	E	S	S
E	N	i	E	R	C	E	P	S	P	T	N	K	T	R
V	S	D	M	T	O	R	E	W	E	B	R	T	i	W
N	H	E	S	T	U	E	F	V	O	O	A	R	R	E
H	A	R	A	H	R	E	S	K	R	S	F	M	F	S
D	G	i	T	R	A	V	i	S	F	O	E	N	L	E
R	Y	S	O	E	G	M	S	P	A	R	K	E	Y	O
E	i	R	E	E	E	O	W	H	M	i	E	L	R	P
A	E	R	E	G	M	T	M	G	i	H	N	H	O	S
M	U	R	E	O	E	C	R	F	L	A	E	A	T	E
S	E	V	V	S	N	S	R	A	Y	H	S	E	O	L
i	L	L	U	S	T	R	A	T	O	R	O	E	Y	i
U	B	i	i	P	D	B	H	Y	F	S	O	T	E	M

Stir-Fly Maze

Help Sparkey get to his favorite dinner...Stir-Fly!

61544695R00024

Made in the USA
Middletown, DE
11 January 2018